JUV/
HV
6773.52
.A465
2001

KING

# Hate and Racist Groups

## Other titles in the *Hot Issues* series

Cult
Awareness
**A Hot Issue**
ISBN 0-7660-1196-8

Cyberdanger and
Internet Safety
**A Hot Issue**
ISBN 0-7660-1368-5

Date
Rape
**A Hot Issue**
ISBN 0-7660-1198-4

Drug Abuse
and Teens
**A Hot Issue**
ISBN 0-7660-1372-3

Eating
Disorders
**A Hot Issue**
ISBN 0-7660-1336-7

Endangered Animals
of North America
**A Hot Issue**
ISBN 0-7660-1373-1

Multiethnic Teens
and Cultural Identity
**A Hot Issue**
ISBN 0-7660-1201-8

Sexually Transmitted
Diseases
**A Hot Issue**
ISBN 0-7660-1192-5

Stalking
**A Hot Issue**
ISBN 0-7660-1364-2

Teens,
Depression,
and the Blues
**A Hot Issue**
ISBN 0-7660-1369-3

Teens and
Pregnancy
**A Hot Issue**
ISBN 0-7660-1365-0

Teen Privacy
Rights
**A Hot Issue**
ISBN 0-7660-1374-X

Teen Smoking and
Tobacco Use
**A Hot Issue**
ISBN 0-7660-1359-6

The Women's
Movement
and Young Women
Today
**A Hot Issue**
ISBN 0-7660-1200-X

# Hate and Racist Groups

## A Hot Issue

Linda Jacobs Altman

**Enslow Publishers, Inc.**

| | |
|---|---|
| 40 Industrial Road | PO Box 38 |
| Box 398 | Aldershot |
| Berkeley Heights, NJ 07922 | Hants GU12 6BP |
| USA | UK |

http://www.enslow.com

Copyright © 2001 by Linda Jacobs Altman

All rights reserved.

No part of this book may be reproduced by any means
without the written permission of the publisher.

**Library of Congress Cataloging-in-Publication Data**

Altman, Linda Jacobs, 1943–
Hate and racist groups : a hot issue / Linda Jacobs Altman.
      p.  cm. — (Hot issues)
Includes bibliographical references and index.
ISBN 0-7660-1371-5 (hard : alk. paper)
1. Hate groups—United States—Juvenile literature.  2. Hate crimes—
United States—Juvenile literature.  [1. Hate groups.  2. Hate crimes.
3. Race relations. 4. Prejudices.]  I. Title.  II. Series.
HV6773.52 .A465 2000
364.1—dc21
    00-008978

Printed in the United States of America

10 9 8 7 6 5 4 3 2 1

**To Our Readers:**
All Internet Addresses in this book were active and appropriate when we
went to press. Any comments or suggestions can be sent by e-mail to
Comments@enslow.com or to the address on the back cover.

**Illustration Credits:** AP/Wide World Photos, pp. 8, 15, 22, 23, 26,
30, 37, 41, 44, 47, 52; Corbis Images Royalty-Free, p. 3; Intelligence
Project/Southern Poverty Law Center, p. 20.

**Cover Illustration:** Corbis Images Royalty-Free

# Contents

# Chapter 1

# Hate on a Crime Spree

**O**n November 19, 1999, a jury in Jasper, Texas, found Shawn Allen Berry guilty of murder. Berry was the last of three white men convicted of a brutal killing. None of them had known the victim, James Byrd, Jr., before the night of the murder. They chose him for one reason: He was black.

It happened before dawn on June 7, 1998. Berry and his companions, Lawrence Russell Brewer and John William King, spotted Byrd walking along the road. They offered him a ride. Then they beat him unconscious and chained his ankles to the back of their pickup truck. They dragged him nearly three miles, over road so rough it ripped Byrd's head from his body.

Police found Byrd's torso dumped beside an African-American church. Byrd's head was nearly a mile away.

Three separate juries in three separate trials found the killers guilty. King and Brewer were sentenced to death. Berry was sentenced to life in prison. He must serve forty years before he can be considered for parole.

*J*ohn William King (front) and Lawrence Russell Brewer are shown being escorted from the Jasper County Jail on June 9, 1998. King, Brewer, and Shawn Allen Berry were later convicted of the brutal murder of James Byrd, Jr. The men had tied Byrd to a truck and dragged him to his death along a rural road in Texas.

The Byrd case shocked the nation. In Texas, it made history. It was the first time a white person had been sentenced to death for killing an African American. Texas journalist Paul Burka called that a "milestone," and wondered whether it represented "how far we have come or how far we have to go."[1]

# Hate Crimes and Bias Incidents: Defining the Problem

Hate, or bias, crimes are acts committed out of prejudice against a particular group of people. The federal government defines a hate crime as one in which "the defendant intentionally selects a victim . . . because of . . . race, color, religion, national origin, ethnicity, gender, disability or sexual orientation."[2]

In 1997, the U.S. Attorney General's office recorded 8,049 hate crimes.[3] Most authorities believe the true number is much higher. Many hate crimes go unreported by victims or unrecognized by police. Victims are often afraid to report such crimes, or they feel that reporting them is useless. Police may not be trained to deal with the prejudices that turn an ordinary crime into a hate crime.

Recognizing hate crimes is not always easy. Proving them in a court of law is even harder. Everything depends on the motive, or reason, for the crime. For example, a group of white teenagers barges into a convenience store and beats up the black clerk. Is that a hate crime? If the offenders attacked the clerk because of his race, then the answer is yes. If they wanted to rob the store and did not care about the clerk's race, then the answer is no.

In addition to the offender's motive, the victim's group is also important. Laws differ from state to state. For example, some states do not include homosexuals or people with disabilities in their protected categories. Nine states have no hate crime laws at all. These differences lead to much confusion. They also raise a number of constitutional issues.

In 1993, Wisconsin's hate crime law was tested before the United States Supreme Court. The case of *Wisconsin* v. *Todd Mitchell* involved a vicious attack on a fourteen-year-old boy. The attackers were African-American. Their victim was white.

DR. M. L KING. JR. BRANCH

# Was the Littleton Massacre a Hate Crime?

April 20, 1999, started as a normal Tuesday at Columbine High School in Littleton, Colorado. Then the killings began. Just before 11:30 A.M., Dylan Klebold and Eric Harris opened fire in the school cafeteria. Then they shot their way through the halls and entered the school library. There they killed twelve students, then turned the guns on themselves.

Including the gunmen, fifteen people died that day.

The Littleton massacre was definitely a terrorist attack. Was it also a hate crime?

**Those who say *yes* point out the following:**

✓Klebold and Harris were fascinated by the racist Nazi regime of World War II Germany. They deliberately chose Adolf Hitler's birthday for their attack.

✓They shouted racial slurs as they killed.

✓They especially targeted African-American student Isaiah Shoels.

**Those who do not think the Littleton massacre fits the legal definition of a hate crime note the following:**

✓Most victims were white.

✓Klebold and Harris seemed more interested in killing student athletes than in killing minorities. During the shootings, one of them yelled, "All jocks stand up! We're going to kill every one of you."[1]

✓African-American victim Isaiah Shoels was also a star athlete. That could have been the chief motive for killing him, not race.

✓The motives of the killers were too complex to categorize.

---

[1]Source: David Foster, "A Penchant for Hate Was a Common Bond: Suspected Killers Openly Admired Hitler, Spoke of War, Guns," *Topeka Capital Journal*, April 22, 1999, <http://cjonline.com/stories/042299/new_shootersbond.shtml> (January 18, 2000).

The crime began with a group of young men hanging around an apartment complex. They were talking about a movie in which a white man beats a black boy. Mitchell turned the conversation from movies to real life with one question: "Do you all feel hyped up to move on some white people?"[4]

A few minutes later, the victim walked by. "There goes a white boy; go get him," Mitchell yelled. He "counted to three and pointed in the boy's direction. The group ran toward the boy, beat him severely, and stole his tennis shoes. The boy was . . . unconscious and remained in a coma for four days."[5]

This offense would usually get two years in prison. Because the motive was racial, Mitchell's sentence went up to seven years. His lawyers appealed, claiming that Wisconsin's hate crime law was unconstitutional.

The U.S. Supreme Court did not agree. On June 11, 1993, the court upheld Mitchell's sentence. It ruled that the Wisconsin law did not punish opinions, which are protected under the constitution. It punished criminal actions, which are not protected.

## The Offenders

The Mitchell case is an example of a thrill crime. This is the most common type of hate crime, accounting for 60 percent of all reported cases.[6] The offenders are typically young males, out looking for excitement. In many of these cases, the attackers "would probably not engage in such behavior on their own," according to hate-crime experts Jack Levin and Jack McDevitt. "[The] leader of a thrill hate crime may be the only member of the group [motivated by] hatred. . . . Most members merely follow along . . . to avoid being rejected [by their friends]."[7]

Thrill-crime offenders attack almost at random. They are not seeking revenge against a group that has specifically done them wrong. Any member of any minority group will do. For example, a gang of young white men might go looking for African Americans to attack. If they do not find any, they might attack a Latino or an Asian person.

This is not the case with offenses known as reactive crimes. Reactive offenders target their victims. They hate blacks, Asians, Latinos, or whomever, because of some real or imagined threat.

Adults are more likely than young people to commit this type of crime. The typical reactive offender is a working-class white male who feels

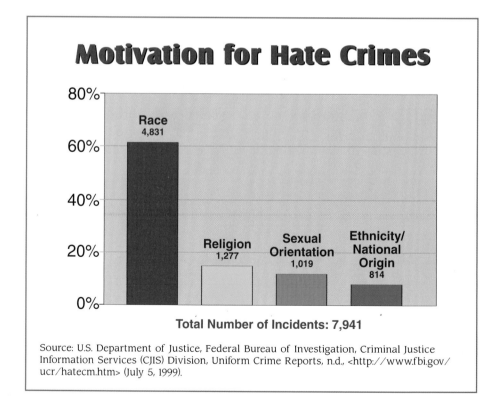

## Motivation for Hate Crimes

Race 4,831

Religion 1,277

Sexual Orientation 1,019

Ethnicity/ National Origin 814

**Total Number of Incidents: 7,941**

Source: U.S. Department of Justice, Federal Bureau of Investigation, Criminal Justice Information Services (CJIS) Division, Uniform Crime Reports, n.d., <http://www.fbi.gov/ucr/hatecm.htm> (July 5, 1999).

overwhelmed by social changes. He is angry and needs someone to blame. Too often, that "someone" is an African-American neighbor or a Jewish coworker. The offender strikes out, claiming that he is defending his way of life against those who would destroy it.

Reactive hate crimes can involve whole communities. For example, in 1991 an economic downturn triggered a wave of hate crimes in a Brooklyn, New York, neighborhood known as Canarsie. The trouble started when housing values plunged and unemployment rates soared. Some whites blamed minorities for the problem. Ethnic tensions grew and soon boiled over into violence.

Levin and McDevitt described the situation in their book, *Hate Crimes*:

> During a twelve-month period, there were more than fifteen racial incidents in Canarsie. Unknown arsonists burned a Pakistani grocery store and firebombed a black-owned insurance office. A local real estate office was firebombed after it showed homes to black families. Then, three black men beat up a twenty-year-old white man after shouting racial slurs at him from their car.[8]

Few reactive- and thrill-crime offenders actually belong to organized hate groups. Their hatred may be strong, but it is not a way of life. Hatred plays a bigger role in the lives of hate group members. Their hate crimes are often of the type known as mission crimes.

Mission crimes are committed by people who believe they are fighting for a cause. They often belong to organizations that want "to rid the world of evil by disposing of the members of a despised group."[9]

Mission hate crimes may range from brawling in the streets to murder and acts of mass terrorism. For example, racist gangs turned the town of Imperial Beach, California, into a war zone. All of San Diego county had been mostly white until the early 1990s. Then Latinos and Asians began moving into the area in large numbers. Experts on population patterns estimated that by 2015, the county's population would be evenly split between whites and nonwhites.

Some whites were afraid of that change. Dan Shorkey was one of them. Rather than live among nonwhites, he decided to move his family to a small town in Georgia. "There's only 68,000 people in the county and it's majority white," he said. "That's where I want to live. That's the way I want to live."[10]

Dan Shorkey did not attack anyone. He just packed up his prejudices and left. Under the Constitution, that was his right. Others in the community joined hate groups and harassed minorities.

A youth gang known as "skinheads" set out to drive nonwhites from the area. They picked fights with minorities and firebombed the home of a Mexican-American family.

The difference between Dan Shorkey and the fire bombers is an important one. It is not against the law to hold racist opinions or even to join a hate group. The United States Constitution guarantees every American the right to free speech, free association, and free assembly. Only those who resort to violence or other criminal acts can be arrested and imprisoned.

## The Victims

Hate crimes terrify victims and terrorize whole communities. Victims are not attacked because of

*A* cross made of rocks now marks the spot where Matthew Shepard was tied to a fence after his attackers fatally beat him.

something they did or did not do. They are attacked because of who they are—something they cannot change. Every member of the victim's group knows that he or she could be next.

As the American Correctional Association noted, "bias crimes continue the oppression of marginalized groups, leaving victims and members of the victims' communities feeling isolated, vulnerable, and unprotected by the law."[11]

For example, in October 1998, the homosexual community was stunned by the brutal killing of a gay college student in Laramie, Wyoming. Two young men lured twenty-one-year-old Matthew Shepard from a bar. They burned him and beat him with the butt of a pistol. Then they tied him to a fence and left him there to die.

Passersby discovered Shepard and summoned help. He was taken to a Fort Collins, Colorado, hospital, where he died on October 13, 1998. Commander Dave O'Malley of the Laramie Police said that Shepard was targeted because he was gay.

Fear spread through gay and lesbian communities all over the country. They held vigils and protest marches. They called for stronger laws against antihomosexual violence.

In Wyoming, the two young men who attacked Matthew Shepard were charged with first-degree murder. They were not charged with a hate crime. Wyoming has no hate crime law.

Minority leaders and civil rights activists hope to change that. They hope that the twenty-first century will be a time when society says *no* to those who hurt people whose only "crime" is being different.

# Chapter 2

# The Many Faces of Hate

There are several kinds of hate groups. Some teach that one race is better than others. Some focus on social and political issues. Some use religion to disguise hatred. These categories are not rigid. In the world of hate groups, there is a great deal of crossover.

For example, militant antiabortionists may join antigovernment "patriot" groups. White supremacists who hate people of color, and anti-Semites who hate Jews, may join racist churches. As these groups feed off one another's hatred, they become more dangerous. Many of them do not hesitate to use terrorism in service to their cause.

Regardless of their beliefs, hate groups have much in common. They exist on the fringes of society, giving their members someplace to belong and someone to hate. They are certain that they are absolutely right—and that anyone who disagrees with them is absolutely wrong.

## The Price of Belonging

Hate groups serve up ready-made ideologies that offer easy answers to some of life's hardest questions. Having those "answers" helps members feel superior to those who are not in their group. Many think that they are the chosen few who have been entrusted with absolute Truth.

Group members do not like having their beliefs challenged by outsiders. Some refuse even to listen to opposing views. Others listen only so that they can "disprove" ideas that do not fit their worldview. Some can discuss their beliefs reasonably until a pointed question makes them uncomfortable. Then they often get angry and put a quick end to the conversation.

Raphael Ezekiel, who is Jewish, had many such conversations when he was studying racist groups. In his book *The Racist Mind*, he tells of a conversation with a man who talked about government conspiracies and Jewish evil.

Ezekiel guessed that this young man had probably never known any Jews. He decided to find out:

"Look," I said, "in real life, I get my ideas about people by what really happens, day by day what really happens with them. Now you, you're from a little town in North Carolina, I reckon."

"No," he answered, "Tennessee."

"Okay," I said, "But the point is, how many Jews were in your town?"

"None," he said. "None. But all I need to know about Jews—" He was shouting by now; he had grabbed his Bible and sprung it open, he thumped it, he lifted it into the air above his head, he slashed the air with it. "All I need to know about Jews, I get it *right here*!" He slammed his hand onto the [Bible]. "All I need to know, *the Book* tells me!"[1]

Just what "the Book" told him, he did not say.

Racists and anti-Semites often use their group's interpretation of the Bible to justify their beliefs.

Members of hate groups often give up their individuality and independent thinking. They tend to "follow the crowd," believing what they are told to believe and doing what they are told to do. In return, many hate groups offer more than a ready-made ideology. There are rallies and marches to attend, books to read, movies to see, and speeches to hear. They provide a total way of life.

For example, every Labor Day weekend, Ku Klux Klan groups gather at Stone Mountain, Georgia. The weather is warm, the mood casual. A steady parade of speakers and music groups bombards the crowd with racist ideas and racist language. A number of

## What Does Hate Mean?

In the dictionary, "hate" means a deep, personal feeling of hostility. In real life, hate means that every day . . .

✓Some people are called hurtful names.

✓Some people are unfairly excluded from jobs, neighborhoods, schools, and clubs.

✓Some people are attacked and beaten.

✓Some people's homes, places of worship, or cemeteries are vandalized.

✓Some people are unfairly paid less than others for doing equal work.

Source: "What to Tell Your Child About Prejudice and Discrimination," Anti-Defamation League & The National PTA, 1999, <http://www.adl.org/default.htm> (6/3/00).

small wooden booths offer racist materials for sale. The vendors display everything from books to bumper stickers. A popular sticker at one Stone Mountain rally read "Praise God for AIDS" (because AIDS is a disease that kills many homosexuals).[2] (AIDS is the final, life-threatening stage of infection with HIV, a virus that greatly weakens the immune system of the infected person.)

The gatherings end with a ritual cross-burning. The members erect a large wooden cross. After dark they gather around it, dressed in their trademark white robes and hoods. Someone sets the cross on fire. The members stand in silence, watching it burn. Some are moved to tears.

The Klan has used the burning cross as a symbol of hatred and terror since the Civil War. According to some Klan leaders, there is a deeper meaning to the ritual: "It's not a cross-burning. It's a cross-*lighting*,"

*M*embers of the original Ku Klux Klan rode by night, wearing white robes and hooded masks. The Ku Klux Klan of today still uses the trademark robes.

said Klan leader Charles Lee. "It represents the light of Jesus Christ in the world."[3]

Jim Stinson, another Klan leader, considered the cross-burning "a call to arms. . . . The old clans of Scotland would signal with burning crosses on the hillsides to call their people. We're doing the same thing—calling our people."[4]

# Spreading the Word

Recruiting new members is important to extremist groups. The desire to grow is not only a matter of numbers. It is a matter of pride. Members see converts as proof that their view of the world is true.

Extremist groups get their messages out in many different ways. They send recruiters into the community. They publish magazines and newspapers and operate telephone information centers. They sponsor radio and television broadcasts.

Former white supremacist Thomas James "T.J." Leyden specialized in recruiting young people. After turning away from racism, he explained his methods to human rights groups and law enforcement agencies: "I targeted junior high schools . . . by [stirring up] fights between white and non-white kids. . . . I passed out racial comics and . . . [racist] leaflets to the young students."[5]

These person-to-person methods worked well, but slowly. Recruiters like Leyden considered themselves lucky to reach a dozen students at a time. Television and radio can reach thousands. Because radio is less expensive than television, it has been the medium of choice.

The end of the Fairness Doctrine in 1987 made radio even more popular with extremist groups. This Federal Communications Commission (FCC) rule

*F*ormer white supremacist Tom "T.J." Leyden was the founder of one of California's first skinhead groups. Leyden now works for peace at the Simon Wiesenthal Museum of Tolerance in Los Angeles.

had required broadcasters to air both sides of controversial issues. According to Robert L. Hilliard and Michael C. Keith in their book *Waves of Rancor*, the ruling "could be applied when a station broadcast only one side of an issue . . . and then refused to honor requests . . . to present opposing viewpoints."[6]

The FCC established the Fairness Doctrine in 1949. In 1987, President Ronald Reagan vetoed a Congressional bill to make the FCC rule into a federal law. Radio and television stations were no longer required to give equal time to both sides of an issue. This opened the airwaves to a flood of extremist programs.

Radio was and is a powerful tool, but in the 1990s the Internet began to overshadow it. The Net is vast and always changing. It is not regulated by any government or owned by any corporation. In the online world, old standards often go by the wayside. Even time and place have no meaning. The Net is available around the clock. People in small country towns can use it as readily as people in big cities.

In 1998, the United States government estimated that Internet usage was "doubling every hundred days, with some 70 million Americans using [it]." The same report noted that "the Internet was growing faster than all previous communication technologies."[7] The Net gained 50 million users in its first four years of existence. By contrast, it took radio thirty-eight years to reach that many people. Television took thirteen years.

Jerry Berman of the Center for Democracy and Technology calls the Net an "electronic, global Gutenberg printing press that turns all citizens into publishers who can reach

*M*any law enforcement agencies are now using the Internet to track and monitor Web sites that belong to hate groups.

thousands and even millions of people around the country and the world."[8] Hate groups were quick to see the Internet's potential. The first hate site went online in 1995. By 1998, there were 254 such sites. By the beginning of the twenty-first century, the Simon Wiesenthal Center had identified over 2,200 "problematic sites" on the Web.[9]

The Net has raised a whole new set of Constitutional issues. The Bill of Rights guarantees free speech, but that does not mean there are no limits at all. As Justice Oliver Wendell Holmes once said, nobody has the right to yell "fire" in a crowded theater. It is illegal to tell harmful lies about someone; the courts call that slander. It is also illegal to start a riot, publish certain types of pornography, or use profanity on television.

It is uncertain just what will happen with the Net. Should it be regulated? If so, how much and by whom? These are the questions society faces in the twenty-first century. While government, the media, and concerned individuals seek answers, hate groups are out there on the Web, reaching an audience that grows bigger every day.

# Chapter 3

# White Supremacy Groups

**F**or white supremacists, race is destiny. Race tells who you are and who you can hope to become. It defines your place in the world.

White supremacist groups have devised several different "plans" for nonwhites and Jews. They range from strict segregation, or separation, to outright extermination. There is even a plan to divide the United States into separate "homelands," or nations. One Ku Klux Klan leader actually drew up a map. It carved the United States into separate "countries" for whites, blacks, Jews, Asians, Latinos, and other minorities.

Today there are dozens of white supremacist groups. They range from the white-robed Ku Klux Klan to neo-Nazis and skinhead gangs. They share a common belief in white superiority. They also share a common fear that Jews and people of color threaten their "racial purity."

## Night Riders: The Ku Klux Klan

Three organizations have carried the name of Ku Klux Klan. The first was founded at Pulaski,

DR. M. L KING. JR RRANCH

Tennessee, after the Civil War. The Klansmen rode by night wearing white robes and hooded masks. They attacked newly freed slaves and any white people who helped them. They flogged, tortured, burned, and hanged their victims. Their reign of terror lasted until the early 1870s, when authorities took action to stop them.

The second Klan was founded in 1915 at a rally on Stone Mountain in Georgia. Organizer William Simmons called upon supporters to take up the cause of white supremacy. This version of the Klan kept the robes and masks along with the "night

*A* member of the Ku Klux Klan taunts protestors at a rally in Greensburg, Pennsylvania, on August 16, 1997. Some protestors threw eggs, bottles, and garbage at Klan members.

rider" image. Secrecy was important. Elaborate rituals and codes surrounded every activity.

For example, a Klansman who wanted to make contact in a new town might ask someone if he knew "Mr. Ayak." If the stranger replied that he knew "Mr. Akia," the visitor would know he had found a kindred spirit. "Ayak" stood for "Are You a Klansman? "Akia" meant "A Klansman I Am."

The new Klan expanded the definition of white supremacy. Simply having white skin was no longer enough. One had to be Anglo-Saxon (of English ancestry), Protestant, and native-born. The second Klan despised Roman Catholics, Jews, and immigrants as well as people of color.

The third version of the Klan began shortly after World War II. It expanded during the civil rights movement of the 1950s and 1960s. While young activists struggled to end racial segregation in the South, the Klan fought to keep it alive.

They used terror tactics to prevent African Americans from going to school with whites, eating in the same restaurants, and riding the same buses. To stop the bombings and murders, President Lyndon Johnson ordered a congressional investigation. Arrests soon followed, and many Klan leaders were held accountable for their crimes.

By the early 1970s, the Klan was floundering. It survived by changing, breaking into dozens of local groups. The hate, the robes, and the burning crosses were still there. The centralized power was not. By the late 1990s, the Klan had become "a loose network of more than 50 splinter groups with perhaps 6,000 members," according to HateWatch director David Goldman.[1]

# Hitler's Heirs:
# The National Alliance

German dictator Adolf Hitler believed that the Germanic and northern European peoples were superior to all others. He also believed that people with genetic, or inborn, flaws should not be allowed to have children. According to Hitler, the disabled, the mentally ill, and the mentally retarded should not even be allowed to live. He dreamed of creating a "master race": strong, dedicated, and ruthless.

In the 1930s and 1940s, he tried to bring that dream to life. First, Hitler's Nazi party began forcing people with inherited flaws to be sterilized so that they could not have children. Next came the killing of handicapped infants, then older children, and then handicapped adults as well.

The final step was genocide, the systematic killing of whole groups of people. Under Adolf Hitler, Nazi Germany exterminated 6 million Jews and 5 million others they considered "inferior." The non-Jewish victims included Poles, Russians, Gypsies, and homosexuals.

World War II put an end to this dark dream. After Germany surrendered in 1945, Hitler's Reich, or empire, lay in ruins. Unfortunately, the ideas that shaped it have survived. They live on in the work of neo-Nazis who dress in Nazi uniforms and greet one another with stiff-armed "Heil Hitler" salutes.

A group called the "National Alliance" openly honors Hitler and accepts Nazi goals as its own. According to the Anti-Defamation League (ADL), the Alliance is "the single most dangerous organized hate group in the United States today."[2] It endorses violence and seeks to do away with democracy, kill or eject minorities, and form an all-white nation. Its

# Words of Hatred

*"Our clear goal must be the advancement of the white race and separation of the white and black races. This goal must include freeing of the American media and government from . . . Jewish interests."*[1]

—David Duke
White supremacist leader

*"The Jews are trying to kill us, and therefore we hate them. It's just that simple."*[2]

—"David Wolfgang Hawke" (Andy Greenbaum)
Jewish student turned neo-Nazi leader

*"Anti-Jew was a big part of what we talked about. . . . People in general want to blame their problems on something; they all want a scapegoat. Blame the Jew, blame the black. I knew how to play him."*[3]

—Brian Lobianco
Former skinhead recruiter

*"[I] walked through town with my gun in my waist, saw the black guy and thought he didn't belong where he was at. How easy it would be to take him out right there. Didn't seem like much to me."*[4]

—Nathan Thill
Skinhead; convicted killer

Sources: [1]"David Duke: In His Own Words," Anti-Defamation League, February 1999, <http://www.adl.org/default.htm> (5/4/00); [2]"Knight of Freedom," Southern Poverty Law Center, 1998, <http://www.splcenter.org/splc.html> (5/4/00); [3]Daniel Voll, "A Few Good Nazis," *Esquire*, vol. 125, April 1, 1996, p. 102; [4]"Denver Skinhead Says It 'Didn't Seem Like Much' to Kill Black Man," *The Dallas Morning News*, November 22, 1997, p. 4A.

leader, William Pierce, is anti-Jewish, antiblack, and antigovernment.

Pierce's novel, *The Turner Diaries*, deals with a group of fanatic Aryans who take over the world. Many consider it a kind of "terrorist manual." It may have inspired the 1995 bombing of the Alfred P. Murrah Federal Building in Oklahoma City. Convicted bomber Timothy McVeigh read the book many times.

# Fortress of Hate: Aryan Nations

The word "Aryan" originally referred to a language grouping, not a racial one. During the Nazi era in Germany, Adolf Hitler gave it a new definition.

*M*embers of the Aryan Nations clashed with protestors at a rally in Coeur d'Alene, Idaho, on July 3, 1999.

Ever since then, white supremacists have claimed the word as their special property. It refers to people of Anglo-Saxon, Scandinavian, Celtic (Irish, Scottish, Breton), or German descent. All other groups are considered by white supremacists to be "inferior." This idea is the foundation of Aryan Nations belief.

The group began in the mid-1970s, when Richard Girnt Butler bought some land near Hayden Lake, Idaho. He built a compound and declared it the "international headquarters of the White race." Aryan Nations has its own racist church and its own private, unofficial army. It runs the Aryan Brotherhood, which recruits prison inmates to the racist cause.

Every year around Hitler's birthday (April 20), Aryan Nations hosts a gathering. Racists from all over the country flock to the compound. They come to learn the ways of terrorism and armed revolt. Many of them do not belong to Aryan Nations. They come from the Klan, the National Alliance, the patriot militias, and the skinhead youth gangs. Richard Butler's programs are open to all types of white supremacists, seeking to unite them into a single force that will do battle for the racist cause.

# Young, White, and Angry: Racist Skinheads

The skinhead movement began in England in the 1970s. It came to the United States in the 1980s. At first, skinhead activity centered around punk rock music and working-class rebellion. Some skinheads kept that focus. Others turned to racism. They became the "shock troops" of the supremacist movement. They were daring, often vicious, and enjoyed violence for its own sake.

Skinheads are mostly teenagers. They like to shock the adult world by shaving their heads and wearing leather bomber jackets and steel-toed boots. Tattoos are a special status symbol. For example, a twenty-two-year-old skinhead in Denver, Colorado, had fifteen different tattoos. His favorite one was the word "carnage," written in huge letters across his back.[3]

The skinhead movement is made up of many independent groups or gangs. Some of them are loosely connected to a group called the White Aryan Resistance (WAR). The head of WAR is Tom Metzger, an ex-Klansman who specializes in recruiting young people. He sees the skinheads as the "youth wing"[4] of the racist cause.

A 1997 Anti-Defamation League press release estimates that there are between twenty-five hundred and thirty-five hundred racist skinheads active in forty states. Members generally range from ages thirteen to twenty-five.[5] Most of them are from a working-class background and have not succeeded at school or at a job. They tend to have poor relationships with their parents and families. However, with their fellow skinheads, they feel important and part of the group.[6]

Skinheads feel superior just because they are white. One of the main reasons people join racist groups is to feel superior. From the Night Riders of the first Klan to the tattooed skinheads of today, racists build themselves up by putting other people down. Many of them believe their actions are inspired not by hatred, but by "white pride."

# Choosing Targets

In the name of white pride, skinheads and other white supremacists may focus on any nonwhite group they see as a threat. The choice of victims often depends on local conditions. The firebombing of a Mexican-American home in Imperial Beach, California, is one example of this. The skinheads who threw the bomb did not form a special "anti-Mexican" hate group. The attackers simply felt threatened by the number of Latinos moving into the area, so they singled out Latinos. If the minorities moving into Imperial Beach had been East Indians or American Indians, then they could just as well have become the targets.

Another example of this local focus occurred in Houston, Texas, where a Klan group terrorized a community of Vietnamese immigrants. The immigrants had built a sizeable fishing fleet on the Gulf of Mexico. The Klan accused them of putting white fishermen out of work.

This adaptability is one reason white supremacists are so dangerous. They can strike anywhere, anytime, against anyone who offends them. Their hatred threatens all efforts to build a society in which racial and other differences are accepted and respected.

# Chapter 4

# Religious Extremists

**M**ost people believe that religion is supposed to teach decency, brotherhood, and love. Racists and anti-Semites do not see it that way. They think tolerance of different beliefs is a weakness. Brotherly love is only for people like them, not for people of color, Jews, or "sinners" such as homosexuals and abortion providers.

Both the World Church of the Creator and the movement known as Christian Identity preach racism. It is a central part of their doctrine. Dozens of small congregations, many with part-time pastors, follow their lead. The result is a religious movement that says racism and hatred are the will of God.

## Fighting a Holy War: The World Church of the Creator

The Church of the Creator (COTC) burst on the extremist scene with a call for a "holy war." Church founder Ben Klassen called it RAHOWA (RAcial HOly WAr):

RAHOWA! In this one word we sum up the total goal and program of not only the Church of the Creator, but of the total White race, and it is this: We take up the challenge. We [prepare] for total war against the Jews and the rest of the . . . mud races of the world. . . . In fact we regard it as . . . the most sacred credo of all.[1]

In the early 1990s, Klassen's church was "one of the most violent hate groups on the radical right,"[2] according to the Anti-Defamation League. It had several hundred members, including chapters in Sweden, Canada, and South Africa.

All of it began to come apart in the spring of 1991. On May 17, COTC "minister" George Loeb killed African-American sailor Harold Mansfield. Loeb was eventually found guilty of first-degree murder and sentenced to life in prison.

**DR. M. L. KING, JR. BRANCH**

## Profiles of Some Extremist Religious Groups

|  | Church of Jesus Christ, Christian | Church of the Creator | Yahweh ben Yahweh (Cult) | Nation of Islam |
|---|---|---|---|---|
| **Founder** | Richard Butler | Ben Klassen | Hulon Mitchell, Jr. (aka Yahweh ben Yahweh) | Wallace Fard Muhammed |
| **Affiliation** | Christian Identity | Church of the Creator | Black Hebrew Israelites | Nation of Islam |
| **Location** | Hayden Lake, Idaho | Peoria, Illinois (headquarters) | Miami, Florida | Various |
| **Belief** | White Supremacist | White Supremacist | Black Supremacist | Black Supremacist |

The Mansfield case led to a $1 million lawsuit against the church. In 1993, leader Ben Klassen killed himself with an overdose of sleeping pills. The Church of the Creator floundered. Chapters disbanded. Members drifted away. Then, in 1996, law-school graduate Matt Hale took over leadership. He added "World" to the church's name and moved the headquarters to his hometown of Peoria, Illinois.

Membership began to grow again. Church recruiters set up active chapters in several cities around the country. By 1998, Hale claimed that WCOTC had nearly three thousand members. The Anti-Defamation League called this "new" version of the church "yet another example of the need for continued [watchfulness] in the fight against violent extremism."[3]

# God's Chosen People: The Christian Identity Movement

Christian Identity tailors its message to the prejudices of its members. For anti-Semites, it teaches that white Anglo-Saxons are the lost tribes of "true" (white) Israel, and that Jews are the children of the devil. For racists, it teaches that people of color were created with the animals; that they may look human, but are not human. It proclaims that nonwhites have no souls; that only white people were born of Adam and Eve, so only white people are truly human.

Such beliefs not only justify racism, they make it seem like a sacred duty. Identity followers see themselves as heroes in a holy cause. They believe that one day they will fight a last, great battle against the forces of Satan. They believe that this evil force will not come from Hell, but from Washington, D.C.

Christian Identity teaches that the United States government is entirely controlled by Jews and racial minorities. They call it the "Zionist Occupational Government" (ZOG). According to them, ZOG is vast and evil. ZOG intends to destroy white America with everything from civil rights laws and welfare programs to legalized abortion.

# Black Backlash: Nation of Islam and Black Hebrew Israelites

White people are not the only ones who have formed religions based upon racial hatred. Some African Americans, enraged by a history that has included slavery, racial segregation, and discrimination at the hands of white people, have formed their own racist religions.

The most violent of these religions is the Black Hebrew Israelite movement. In the 1980s, a Black Hebrew Israelite group in Miami, Florida, launched a reign of terror that left fourteen people dead. Most of the victims were white. They were picked at random and killed because of their race. Some of those killed were black people who were considered "traitors" to the movement.

*N*ation of Islam leader Louis Farrakhan spoke to followers at the group's Saviour's Day Convention on February 23, 1997. In his speech, Farrakhan said that blacks should form a nation of their own.

Black Hebrew Israelites believe that God is black and that they are his chosen people. They believe that white people are "devils," and Jews the children of Satan. The resemblance to Christian Identity is unmistakable. Even WAR leader Tom Metzger calls the Black Hebrew Israelites "the black counterpart of us."[4]

The Nation of Islam also has much in common with the white supremacist movement. It teaches that blacks are God's chosen people. It proclaims that whites are "'blue-eyed devils' created by an evil scientist named Yacub as a laboratory experiment."[5]

Nation of Islam leader Reverend Louis Farrakhan is well known for his antiwhite and anti-Semitic views. Many blacks and whites consider him a racist who despises nonblacks, a sexist who considers women inferior to men, and a homophobe who hates gays. His call for racial separatism would not be out of place in a Christian Identity church.

However strange and terrible hate-based religions may seem, they confront the same questions that trouble everybody else. People turn to them for answers to some of life's most important questions. Their members want to know about good and evil, life and death, and the meaning of existence. They want to feel that there is a God somewhere who loves them.

It is not the questions that make hate-based religions different and dangerous. It is their answers. These churches seek to divide people rather than unite them in a common bond of brotherly love.

# Chapter 5

# The Patriot Militias

The word "patriot" makes many Americans think of people like George Washington, Thomas Jefferson, and John Adams. The extremists who call themselves patriots today have nothing in common with these founding fathers. The patriot movement that began in the 1990s is a loose network of antigovernment militias and hate groups.

Patriot hate lists go beyond the categories included in most hate-crime laws. In addition to nonwhites, non-Christians, and homosexuals, patriots may target abortion providers, the United Nations, and various agencies of the United States government. They believe that all "true Americans" must save their country from what they call the "Zionist Occupational Government" (ZOG).

Patriots claim that ZOG is working with the United Nations to destroy America's national identity. They are sure that every treaty or trade agreement with another country is a step toward the dreaded "New World Order"—a global government under control of the United Nations.

The patriot movement was not seen as an important threat until the early 1990s. Two events focused public attention on these groups, as "Ruby Ridge" and "Waco" became the rallying cries that pulled the extremist right together.

# Shoot-out at Ruby Ridge: The Randy Weaver Case

The place known as Ruby Ridge is a semiwilderness area in the Selkirk Mountains of Northern Idaho. It was here, in August 1992, that three federal marshals placed Randy Weaver under surveillance, or close watch.

Weaver had been arrested on firearms violations and ordered to appear for trial in February 1991. Instead of obeying that order, he holed up on Ruby Ridge. By August 1992, he had been there for eighteen months with his wife and children.

The marshals knew that Randy and Vicki Weaver were white supremacists with ties to Aryan Nations. That meant they almost certainly had weapons. The question was how many and what kind. This was the reason for the surveillance. The marshals wanted to know what to expect before they tried to make an arrest. They hid in the brush and waited.

It was Weaver's dog that gave them away. When it started barking, Weaver went to investigate. His friend Kevin Harris and his fourteen-year-old son Sammy went with him. All of them carried guns.

No one knows exactly how the shooting started. One of the first bullets hit the dog, then both sides opened fire. Kevin Harris killed Deputy Marshal William Degan with a shotgun blast to the chest. In a hail of bullets, Randy Weaver ran back toward the cabin, calling for the others to follow. Sammy never

*A*fter Randy Weaver surrendered to authorities, federal agents and the media inspected the outside of his home. Confiscated guns and ammunition were displayed on the ground.

made it. He fell facedown in the dirt, a fatal bullet in his back.

With two dead already, the marshal's office called in the Federal Bureau of Investigation (FBI). They arrived with an arsenal of weapons and a shoot-to-kill order. When they saw three adults come out into the yard, they opened fire. Weaver, Harris, and Weaver's nineteen-year-old daughter Sara scrambled back toward the cabin, yelling for help.

Vicki Weaver ran to the door with her ten-month-old daughter in her arms. As she stood screaming for the others to get inside, a bullet struck her in the head. She fell to the floor dead, the baby still clasped in her arms.

After Ruby Ridge, a Senate committee criticized the FBI's handling of the case. There had been mistakes, the committee said. The FBI had made serious errors in judgment. On the basis of these findings, Attorney General Janet Reno issued new rules about the use of shoot-to-kill orders.

The patriots were not satisfied. "It was murder, plain and simple," said Klansman Jim Stinson. "Who's going to take responsibility for that? Who's going to be charged with killing Vicki Weaver?"[1]

In October, Christian Identity pastor Pete Peters hosted a three-day conference at Estes Park, Colorado. It was time to unify against the government, he said. Ruby Ridge proved it. In an "Open Letter to the Weaver Family," the group declared its intentions:

> [Motivated] by the spirit of our HEAVENLY FATHER, and hearing the cry of innocent blood shed in the land, WE, 160 Christian men assembled for three days of prayer and counsel.

... We are determined to [use] HIS strength and to work continually to insure that Vicki and Samuel's mortal sacrifices were not in vain.[2]

# Flames of Hatred: The Branch Davidian Case

Barely six months after Ruby Ridge, a little-known religious cult called the Branch Davidians ran into trouble with the law. In their fortress-like headquarters near Waco, Texas, they had gathered a huge stockpile of weapons. Their leader David Koresh (born Vernon Dean Howell) told them they were preparing for the end of the world.

On February 28, 1993, agents from the Bureau of Alcohol, Tobacco and Firearms (ATF) raided the compound. They planned to seize the illegal weapons and arrest David Koresh. The Branch Davidians fired on them, starting a fierce gun battle that left ten people dead. That was the beginning of a standoff that lasted for fifty-one days.

By April 19 government forces had run out of patience. They attacked the compound with tanks and tear gas. Fires broke out in the buildings. Before anyone knew what was happening, the compound was a blazing inferno.

Ninety-six people died in the fire. Seventeen of them were children under the age of five. Investigators were never quite sure how the fire began. The Davidians may have set it themselves, choosing suicide over surrender.

Once more, the patriots shouted "conspiracy." The Waco fire was not a mass suicide, they said. It was a mass murder. Citizens were being slaughtered by their own government for holding unpopular opinions.

*F*lames engulfed the Branch Davidian compound in Waco, Texas, on April 19, 1993, as federal agents tried to drive members out of the buildings.

Attorney Linda Thompson, one of the few women leaders in the patriot movement, took Waco as her special cause. She produced two videos, *Waco: The Big Lie* and *Waco II: The Lie Continues*. These videos claimed to expose the government plot that led to the Branch Davidian fire. They helped make the Waco tragedy a recruiting tool for the extremist right.

## Beliefs of the Patriot Movement

The patriot movement thrives on conspiracy theories. In their world, the enemy is always nearby, hatching plots against the health, safety, and freedom of white America.

Many conspiracy theories center around technology, proposing such ideas as mysterious black helicopters that spy on people or implanted microchips that replace other forms of personal identification. Other theories involve older enemies, such as Jews plotting to control the world through international banking, black people "polluting" the Aryan race through intermarriage, or United Nations troops training for an invasion of America.

Many patriots believe that the only way to avoid these "evils" is to drop out of the society that produces them. Patriots may refuse to pay taxes, license their cars, get a Social Security number, or allow their children to attend public schools. They deny the authority of the police, the courts, and even most of the United States Constitution.

They denounce the whole legal system in favor of something they call "common law." It is a combination of ideas from the Bible, the Bill of Rights, and other sources. Patriot common law usually assumes white superiority. It treats their version of Christianity as the only true religion. It also imposes harsh penalties for abortion, homosexuality, racial intermarriage, and other "criminal" behaviors.

One aspect of this patriot desire for isolation involves survivalism. Survivalists store up supplies and weapons for the day when they will fight the forces of ZOG and the New World Order. Some build their own communities where they try to live without relying on outside sources. They often grow their own food, make their own clothes, and dig their own wells for water.

One of the oldest survivalist settlements is Elohim City. (*Elohim* is a Hebrew name for God.) It is tucked away in the Ozark Mountains of Arkansas.

Founder Robert Millar believes that Jesus "was Aryan . . . a blond Messiah [who] would soon return to redeem a small remnant of the white race."[3]

Elohim City is not completely self-sufficient. According to journalist Vincent Coppola,

> [There] are 50 people inhabiting Elohim City. . . . They live in wood-frame houses and beat-up trailers clustered around the temple. Despite their . . . desire to "keep out of the system," a number are collecting food stamps. The camp has electricity, running water, even a few TV antennas. . . . The men drink an occasional beer [and] the women wear lipstick and modern clothes.[4]

Combat training is also popular with survivalists. The patriot movement has attracted former military and law enforcement people who pass on their skills to others. One of the most popular instructors is former Green Beret James "Bo" Gritz.

A typical advertisement for Gritz's class promises that students will "fire the latest Ruger semi-automatic pistols equipped with laser and red dot sights. Both street confrontation and deliberate shooting will be taught along with instinctive 'Quick Kill' skills. All guns and ammo will be furnished."[5]

In addition to weapons training and combat skills, many patriot groups study the ways of terrorism. At the Estes Park meeting of October 1992, Aryan Nations official Louis Beam presented a plan for small, independent assault units. He called the plan "leaderless resistance."

# Strategies for Terrorism

Leaderless resistance groups, or "cells" as Louis Beam called them, might have only five or six members. There would be no elected leaders, no marches or rallies or chain of command. The cells would not even be known to each other.

Some cells might be basically permanent. Others could be temporary groups formed for a special purpose. When that purpose was accomplished, the group could disband, and its members would go their separate ways. Beam's suggestion was not new. Guerilla fighters (small bands operating inside enemy territory) have used this approach for years. Louis Beam simply adapted the strategy for white supremacist groups.

Former American Nazi Party member Richard Kelly Hoskins took the idea of independent terrorism a step further. He called for attacks by individuals "who feel they are called by God."[6]

*T*he bombing of the Alfred P. Murrah Federal Building in Oklahoma City on April 19, 1995, was the deadliest terrorist act ever committed on American soil.

Terrorism experts call individual attackers such as these "lone wolves."

The lone wolf and the leaderless cell became part of the new face of racist terrorism in the 1990s. Many authorities believe that the rise in lone-wolf terrorism is partly connected to the development of the Internet. As journalist Jo Thomas noted, hate groups use the Internet to "provide the philosophical framework. Individuals with few or no . . . connections to these groups [may] do the killing."[7]

The late 1990s produced many examples of this type of terrorism. The 1995 bombing of the federal building in Oklahoma City was the deadliest terrorist act ever committed on American soil. One hundred and sixty-eight people died in the blast. The bombers, Timothy McVeigh and Terry Nichols, had connections to the neo-Nazi National Alliance.

The August 1999 attack on a Jewish community center near Los Angeles was done by one man, Buford O'Neal Furrow, Jr. Shortly before eleven o'clock on the morning of August 10, Furrow entered the building and opened fire, wounding five people. After fleeing the center he shot and killed a Filipino-American mail carrier. Furrow was described by journalists and police investigators as "a loner with a history of mental health problems and association with racist groups."[8]

The increase in lone-wolf terrorism and the rise of extremist "patriot" groups has frightened many people. Politicians, law enforcement officers, and average citizens debate the meaning of this shadow world. What does it mean for the future? After Oklahoma City, patriot spokesman Bob Fletcher answered that question in three words: "Expect more bombs."[9]

# Chapter 6

# Breaking the Chain of Hate

America was once a mostly white, Christian culture. People of color and non-Christians were clearly in the minority. In the twenty-first century that is likely to change. People who study population patterns estimate that by the year 2050, white and nonwhite populations in America will be nearly equal. As time passes, the United States is becoming more and more a multi-racial, multicultural society.

Most people believe that bigotry and prejudice have no place in such a society, and that people must work together to oppose hatred and promote tolerance. They feel it is not just a matter of morality—it is a matter of survival.

## Putting Hate on Trial

In November 1988, racist skinheads in Portland, Oregon, killed Ethiopian student Mulugeta Seraw. Years later, that murder would produce a landmark case in the struggle against hate crime.

Under criminal law, only the actual killers could be tried for the murder. Tom Metzger's White Aryan

DR. M. L KING, JR. BRANCH

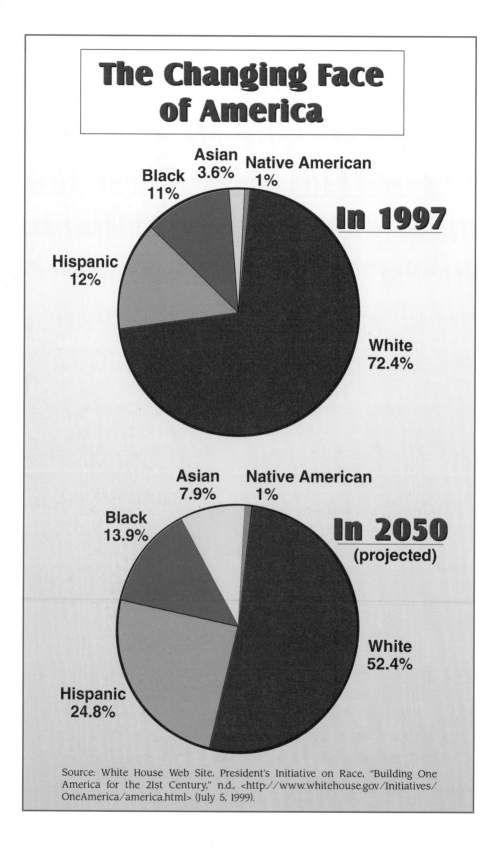

# The Changing Face of America

**In 1997**

Native American 1%
Asian 3.6%
Black 11%
Hispanic 12%
White 72.4%

**In 2050**
(projected)

Native American 1%
Asian 7.9%
Black 13.9%
Hispanic 24.8%
White 52.4%

Source: White House Web Site, President's Initiative on Race, "Building One America for the 21st Century," n.d., <http://www.whitehouse.gov/Initiatives/ OneAmerica/america.html> (July 5, 1999).

Resistance, which had recruited and trained them, could not be charged with any crime. Attorney Morris Dees of the Southern Poverty Law Center filed a civil suit on behalf of Mulugeta Seraw's family.

Criminal law deals with crime and punishment. Civil law deals with responsibility for harm done to another. In criminal cases, offenders can be found guilty and go to prison. In civil cases, they can be found responsible and ordered to pay money damages to the people they have hurt.

Morris Dees's suit claimed that Tom Metzger and his organization were as responsible for Seraw's death as the skinheads who did the actual killing. In October 1990, a jury agreed and awarded over $12 million in damages to the Seraw family.

Metzger appealed the judgment. The case was tied up in court until 1994, when the United States Supreme Court refused to consider Metzger's case any further. This left the judgment standing. The WAR case laid the groundwork for other civil actions that would hold racist groups responsible for the acts of terrorism they inspire.

In the 1990s, civil cases bankrupted several Klan groups and put them out of business. In January 1999, Morris Dees took on Richard Butler and Aryan Nations. He sued for damages on behalf of Victoria Kennan and her nineteen-year-old son Jason. The suit claimed that Aryan Nations members assaulted the Kennans on a public road outside the Hayden Lake compound.

The effect on Butler's operation was immediate. Aryan Nations lost its nonprofit mailing privileges. According to an article in the *Atlanta Constitution*, Butler was forced to appeal for money on the

*D*emonstrators protested a scheduled neo-Nazi march in Washington, D.C., on August 7, 1999. Organizers canceled the march when only four supporters showed up.

Internet and put the Hayden Lake compound up for sale.[1]

# "Not in Our Town You Don't"

In Sacramento, California, they called it the night of fire. Arsonists torched three synagogues in the predawn hours of June 18, 1999. The community responded immediately. Even before investigators left the scene, people began appearing. They came to offer their sympathy and to show solidarity with the Jewish community.

Three days after the attack, a mass gathering drew over four thousand people of every race and creed. Muslim League president Metwalli B. Amer said, "How beautiful to see members of the . . . inter-faith family. How beautiful to see members of the various ethnicities in this radiant community of ours. How beautiful to see the people of our Sacramento County showing their solidarity."[2]

Solidarity is important in the face of hate crimes. Gatherings like the one in Sacramento allow people to express their outrage and sorrow. They also let offenders know that such crimes will not be tolerated.

Solidarity gatherings are a favorite tactic of antihate groups. Many communities hold counter-demonstrations when a hate group comes to town. The most effective of these not only make a statement, they make the hate group defeat its own purpose. For example, a group in Springfield, Illinois, transformed a Ku Klux Klan rally into a fundraiser for the NAACP, Anti-Defamation League, and Southern Poverty Law Center. The event was called "Project Lemonade" after the saying, "When life gives you a lemon, make lemonade." Donors pledged money

DR. M. L. KING, JR BRANCH

for each minute the Klan rally lasted. The longer the rally, the more money the Klan put into the treasuries of its enemies.

A community in Madison, Wisconsin, tried a touch of humor. When Bill and Lindy Seltzer heard that the Klan was planning a rally, they organized a joyous gathering in support of tolerance:

> Nearly 400 people raised banners late in the morning and marched down State Street to the beat of a bass drum. They waved signs that said things like "My What White Hoods You Have!" and chanted "Whose streets? Our streets!"[3]

Some of the Madison marchers made fun of the Klan by parading in blue-and-red polka-dotted sheets as the "Ku Klux Klowns."[4]

Hate groups tend to take themselves very seriously. Poking fun at them makes them look ridiculous, which they do not care for. In the Madison case, once again, an antihate group scored a victory: The Klan actually canceled its own event.

# What You Can Do

Young people can do many things to work against hate, either in groups or as individuals. The following suggestions are adapted from "One America in the 21st Century: The President's Initiative on Race."[5]

➤ Learn about other races and cultures.

➤ Think about your feelings toward people who are different.

➤ Get to know people of other groups.

➤ Speak up when you hear prejudiced comments or see prejudiced actions.

➤ Talk with others about ways to build intergroup harmony.

➤ Support institutions and businesses that promote equality.

➤ Volunteer for community projects that promote multicultural understanding.

➤ Encourage multicultural and ethnic studies programs at school.

Ideas like these will not change the world overnight. Bigotry and prejudice are too deeply rooted in our culture. They grow from the fear of those who are different and from the need to feel better than others.

People who join hate groups and commit hate crimes live in an us-and-them kind of world. People of good will cannot afford to do that. Like it or not, America is fast becoming a multicultural society. Finding ways to overcome our prejudices and make that society work will perhaps be the greatest challenge of the new millennium.

DR. M. L. KING, JR. BRANCH

**Anti-Defamation League**
823 U.N. Plaza
New York, NY 10017
(212) 490-2525

**Facing History and Ourselves**
16 Hurd Rd.
Brookline, MA 02146
<http://info_boston@facing.org>

**President's Initiative on Race:**
**One America in the 21st Century**
The White House
1600 Pennsylvania Ave.
Washington, DC 20500
<http://www.whitehouse.gov/Initiatives/OneAmerica/
america.html>

**Simon Wiesenthal Center**
9760 W. Pico Blvd.
Los Angeles, CA

**Southern Poverty Law Center**
400 Washington Ave.
Montgomery, AL 36104
<http://www.splcenter.org/splc.html>

## Chapter 1. Hate on a Crime Spree

1. Paul Burka, "James Byrd, Jr. The hate-crimes bill bearing his name was supposed to be his legacy. It still may be," *Texas Monthly*, September 1999, <http://www.texasmonthly.com/mag/1999/sep/byrd.html> (January 22, 2000).

2. Elena Grigera, "Hate Crimes: State and Federal Response to Bias-Motivated Violence," American Correctional Association, 1999, n.d., <http://www.corrections.com/aca/cortoday/august99/hatecrimes.html> (January 20, 2000).

3. Eric M. Holder, Jr., quoted in U.S. Senator Orrin Hatch (R-UT), "Chairman U.S. Senator Orrin Hatch (R-UT) Holds Hearing on Hate Crimes," Washington Transcript Service, May 11, 1999, in Electric Library, <www.elibrary.com> (June 12, 1999).

4. Quoted in Supreme Court of the United States, *Wisconsin, Petitioner* v. *Todd Mitchell*. Legal Information Institute and Project Hermes, opinion rendered June 11, 1993, <http://supct.law.cornell.edu/supct/html/92-515.ZS.html> (June 14, 1999).

5. Ibid.

6. Arnold Aronson, "From Hate to Hurt: The Scope of the Problem," *Cause for Concern: Hate Crimes in America*, Leadership Conference Education Fund, May 11, 1995, <http://www.civilrights.org/lcef/hate/toc.html> (June 12, 1999).

7. Jack Levin and Jack McDevitt, *Hate Crimes: The Rising Tide of Bigotry and Bloodshed* (New York: Plenum Press, 1993), pp. 65–66.

8. Ibid., p. 83.

9. Quoted in "The Motives Behind Hate," Media Awareness Network, n.d., <http://www.media-awareness.ca/eng/> (January 28, 2000).

10. Quoted in Associated Press, "Coast Town Is Plagued by Racism," *Sacramento Bee*, November 13, 1996, p. A3.

11. Grigera.

## Chapter 2. The Many Faces of Hate

1. Raphael S. Ezekiel, *The Racist Mind: Portraits of American Neo-Nazis and Klansmen* (New York: Viking Books, 1995), p. 13.

2. Ibid., p. 9.

3. Quoted in Howard L. Bushart, John R. Craig, and Myra Barnes, *Soldiers of God: White Supremacists and Their Holy War for America* (New York: Kensington Publishing Co., 1998), p. 160.

4. Ibid.

5. Ibid.

6. Robert L. Hilliard and Michael C. Keith, *Waves of Rancor: Tuning In the Radical Right.* (Armonk, N.Y.: M.E. Sharpe, 1999), p. 16.

7. Ibid., p. 87.

8. Testimony of Jerry Berman, Executive Director, Center for Democracy and Technology, before the Senate Judiciary Committee, Subcommittee on Terrorism, Technology and Government Information. Quoted in Arnold Aronson, "From Hate to Hurt: The Scope of the Problem," *Cause for Concern: Hate Groups in America*, May 11, 1995, <http://www. civilrights.org/lcef/hate/toc.html> (June 12, 1999).

9. "Hate in America Today," *Response*, Summer/Fall 1999, vol. 20, no. 2, p. 3.

## Chapter 3. White Supremacy Groups

1. Phil Brinkman, "Ku Klux Klan Factions Strive for Attention—Groups Cannot be Overlooked, Say KKK Experts," *Wisconsin State Journal*, January 15, 1999, p. 3A.

2. "Explosion of Hate: The Growing Danger of the National Alliance," New York: Anti-Defamation League, 1998, n.d., <http://www.adl.org/explosion_ of_hate/front_introduction.html> (June 22, 1999).

3. "Skinheads Put Police on Learning Mission: Preoccupied With Gangs They Know, Cops Rush to Get Up to Speed on Newer, Quieter Threat," *Rocky Mountain News*, December 29, 1997, p. 10A.

4. James Ridgeway, *Blood in the Face: The Ku Klux Klan, Aryan Nations, Nazi Skinheads, and the Rise of a New White Culture* (New York: Thunder's Mouth Press, 1995), p. 187.

5. "Skinheads Continue to Pose Threat to Communities in this Country," Anti-Defamation League, December 1, 1997, n.d., <http://www.adl.org/default.htm> (June 23, 1999).

6. Jack Levin and Jack McDevitt, *Hate Crimes: The Rising Tide of Bigotry and Bloodshed* (New York: Plenum Press, 1993), p. 105.

## Chapter 4. Religious Extremists

1. Quoted in "Recurring Hate: Matt Hale and the World Church of the Creator," Anti-Defamation League, 1998, n.d., <http://www.adl.org/default.htm> (June 25, 1999).

2. Ibid.

3. Ibid.

4. Quoted in "Rough Waters: 'Stream of Knowledge' Probed by Officials," Southern Poverty Law Center, *Intelligence Report*, Fall 1997, <http://www.splcenter.org/splc.html> (June 28, 1999).

5. Jonah Blank, "The Muslim Mainstream," *U.S. News & World Report*, vol. 125, July 20, 1998, p. 22.

## Chapter 5. The Patriot Militias

1. Howard L. Bushart, John R. Craig, and Myra Barnes, *Soldiers of God: White Supremacists and Their Holy War for America* (New York: Kensington Publishing Co., 1998), p. 17.

2. Michael Barkun, *Religion and the Racist Right: The Origins of the Christian Identity Movement* (Chapel Hill, N.C.: University of North Carolina Press, 1997), p. 267.

3. Vincent Coppola, *Dragons of God: A Journey Through Far-Right America* (Atlanta: Longstreet Press, Inc., 1996), p. 132.

4. Ibid., p. 137.

5. Bo Gritz, *Center for Action*, September 1993, quoted in Robert Crawford, Steven Gardiner, and Jonathan Mozzuchi, "Almost Heaven?," *The Dignity Report*, March 1994, p. 3.

6. Jo Thomas, "New Face of Terror Crimes: 'Lone Wolf' Weaned on Hate." *The New York Times*, August 16, 1999, pp. A1, A16.

7. Ibid.

8. Laura Mecoy, "Race Cited As a Motive for Slaying," *The Sacramento Bee*, August 13, 1999, p. A1.

9. Quoted in *False Patriots: The Threat of Anti-government Extremists.* (Montgomery, Ala.: Southern Poverty Law Center, 1996), p. 3.

## Chapter 6. Breaking the Chain of Hate

1. Marlon Manuel, "Neo-Nazis Next Target of Lawyer Who Broke Klan," *The Atlanta Constitution*, March 5, 1999, p. C1.

2. Quoted in "All Together Now," *The Sacramento Bee*, June 27, 1999, p. Forum 1.

3. Ron Seely, "Hundreds gather to fight unseen enemy—Klan's absence didn't stop rally—Downtown march, meeting target fight against racism," *Wisconsin State Journal*, January 17, 1999, p. 1A.

4. Ibid.

5. "One America in the 21st Century: The President's Initiative on Race," The White House, 1997, <http://www.whitehouse.gov/Initiatives/OneAmerica/about.html> (February 2, 2000).

**anti-Semitism**—Hatred and/or fear of Jews as a group.

**bias**—A fixed attitude for or against something or someone.

**bigotry**—Dislike of all members of a particular group. Considering other groups to be inferior to one's own.

**conspiracy**—A secret plan for unlawful activity.

**conspiracy theory**—The idea that a given event is the product of an elaborate conspiracy.

**discrimination**—Acting unfairly toward members of a particular group because of prejudices against that group.

**extremism**—Carrying something to excess; "going too far."

**genocide**—The systematic killing of an entire group of people.

**guerilla fighters**—Small bands of soldiers who fight behind enemy lines.

**homophobia**—Hatred and/or fear of homosexuals.

**motive**—The reason for committing a given act.

**prejudice**—Pre-judging. Judging all members of a particular group on the basis of stereotypes.

**racism**—Prejudice or discrimination based on race. The belief that one's own race is superior to others.

**radical**—One who favors fundamental changes in society.

**reactionary**—One who resists change and wants to go back to older ways.

**scapegoating**—Blaming a person or an entire group for something when there is actually no single person or group responsible.

**sexism**—Prejudice or discrimination based on gender.

**stereotype**—An oversimplified "picture" that is supposed to describe all members of a particular group.

**terrorism**—Unlawful acts of violence intended to create fear and alarm. Often committed in support of political causes; for example, to overthrow a government or to destroy certain groups within a society.

Carnes, Jim. *Us & Them: A History of Intolerance in America*. New York: Oxford University Press, Inc., 1996.

Garza, Hedda. *African Americans & Jewish Americans: A History of Struggle*. New York: Franklin Watts, Inc., 1995.

Gay, Kathlyn. *Neo-Nazis: A Growing Threat*. Springfield, N.J.: Enslow Publishers, Inc., 1997.

Gay, Kathlyn. *Rights & Respect: What You Need to Know About Gender & Sexual Harassment*. Brookfield, Conn.: Millbrook Press, 1995.

McDonald, Laughlin, et al. *The Rights of Racial Minorities*. Madison, Wis.: Demco Media, 1998.

Tatum, Beverly Daniel, Ph.D. *Why Are All the Black Kids Sitting Together in the Cafeteria?* New York: Harper Collins, 1999.

Wormser, Richard. *Rise & Fall of Jim Crow: The African-American Struggle Against Discrimination: 1865–1954*. New York: Franklin Watts, Inc., 1999.

Further Reading